Beyond The

CODE

Comprehension and
Reasoning Skills

BOOK 1

Nancy M. Hall

Illustrated by Hugh Price

Educators Publishing Service, Inc.
Cambridge and Toronto

Educators Publishing Service
800.225.5750
www.epsbooks.com

Printed in U.S.A.
ISBN 0-8388-2401-3

4 5 6 7 8 CUR 07 06 05 04 03

Contents

Introduction to **Zack the Dog** PART 1

• Word families can make reading easy. Read the words
below. Blend the letters to make new words. Circle the parts
that are the same.

If you can read **as**, you can read:

(ask)
m(ask)
t(ask)

go
no
so

tell
well
swell
smell
spell

be
he
me
we
she

nag
wag
rag
drag

dust
just
must
rust

1

Words for **Zack the Dog** PART 1

1. **play** =

    It is fun to **play**.   Write and spell it: _____

    stay = s t + A (**Stay** rhymes with **play**.)
    We will **stay** on the bus.

    Write and spell it: _____

    day = d + A (**Day** rhymes with **play**.)
    It is a hot **day**.   Write and spell it: _____

2. **eat** =

    Zack will not **eat**.   Write and spell it: _____

3. **tail** =

    The dog wags its **tail**.   Write and spell it: _____

4. **why** = **Why** rhymes with *I*.
    Zack is sad. **Why** is he sad?

    Write and spell it: _____

5. **give** = giv

    He **gives** me 5¢.   Write and spell it: _____

Read the word list again.

Words for **Zack the Dog** PART 1

• Find the picture that goes with the sentence, and draw a line
  to connect them.

The cat has no **tail**.

Bud **eats** a lot.

Tiz can **stay** and **play** to·day.

Why did the pig miss the bus?

I will **give** Zack a pill.

Means the Same

• Sometimes two words mean the same or nearly the same.
Draw a line from a word in the first list to a word in the
second list that means nearly the same.

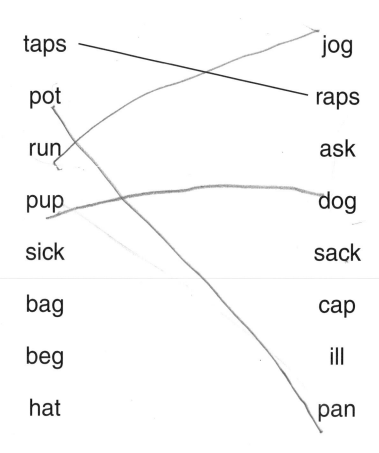

Pick a word from the lists and write a sentence.

_____

_ _

_____

Zack the Dog PART 1

Zack, the pup, is sad.

He will not wag his tail.

Zack, the pup, is sad.

He will not run. He will not play.

He just sits and will not eat.

You can tell; Zack is not a bit well.

Is Zack sick? Is he ill?

Will Miss Pim give him a pill?

Zack, the dog, is Miss Pim's pet.

She has no kids . . . just her pal, Zack.

Miss Pim gives Zack lots to eat.

She hugs him and pats him

And tells him he is swell.

If Zack is sad, you can tell, Miss Pim is sad as well.

But why is Zack sad?

Why has he no get-up-and-go?

Miss Pim can not tell.

She nags him to eat. She begs him to run.

He will not eat. He will not run.

Zack is not a bit of fun!

Miss Pim asks if Zack is sick . . . if he is well.

But Zack just sits and will not tell!

Yes 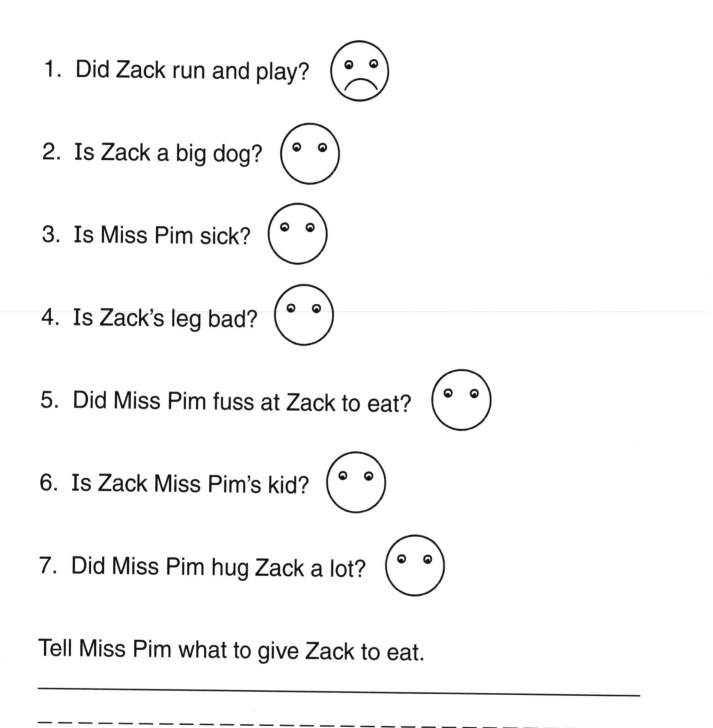 **No** **Can't Tell**

• Draw the face to show the answer.

1. Did Zack run and play?

2. Is Zack a big dog?

3. Is Miss Pim sick?

4. Is Zack's leg bad?

5. Did Miss Pim fuss at Zack to eat?

6. Is Zack Miss Pim's kid?

7. Did Miss Pim hug Zack a lot?

Tell Miss Pim what to give Zack to eat.

_____

_ _

_____

8

Put eyes 👁👁 and a collar → 🐕 on Zack, the pup.
Color it.

Think About It!

1. Name a thing that has 4 legs but is not a dog.
    _____
    -
    _____

2. Name 1 thing you can hug.
    _____
    -
    _____

3. Why is Miss Pim sad?
    _____
    -
    _____

4. Zack has no "get-up-and-go" means:
    _____
    -
    _____

5. Zack is not fat. Can you tell why?
    _____
    -
    _____

6. Why is Zack no fun?
    _____
    -
    _____

Can You Figure This Out?

• The words on each line rhyme. Write 1 more word
  on each line that rhymes.

1. tack   hack   lack   <u>back</u>

2. tug   jug   mug   _____

3. met   let   vet   _____

4. tag   nag   sag   _____

5. man   fan   tan   _____

6. cut   rut   jut   _____

7. mat   cat   rat   _____

Introduction to **Zack the Dog** PART 2

- Contractions are shortcuts. They make words fast and easy to say. Read the 2 words and the contraction. Cross out the letter(s) that were left out in the contraction.

he + i̸s = he's   it + is = it's

she + has = she's   it + will = it'll

- Now read some more word families, and circle the parts that are the same.

If you can read **ill**, you can read:

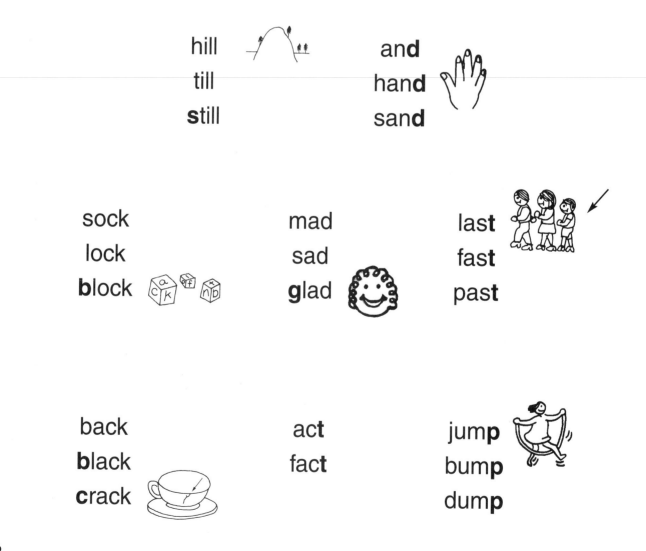

hill   and

till   han**d**

still   san**d**

sock   mad   last

lock   sad   fast

block   **g**lad   pa**st**

back   act   jum**p**

black   fact   bum**p**

crack   dum**p**

Words for **Zack the Dog** PART 2

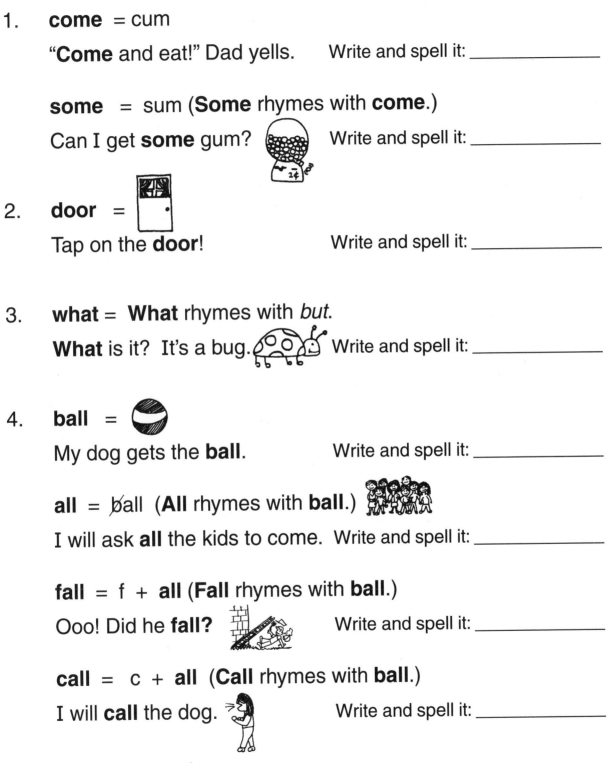

1. **come** = cum

    "**Come** and eat!" Dad yells.   Write and spell it: _____

    some = sum (**Some** rhymes with **come**.)

    Can I get **some** gum?   Write and spell it: _____

2. **door** =

    Tap on the **door**!   Write and spell it: _____

3. **what** = **What** rhymes with *but*.

    What is it? It's a bug.   Write and spell it: _____

4. **ball** =

    My dog gets the **ball**.   Write and spell it: _____

    all = b̸all (**All** rhymes with **ball**.)

    I will ask **all** the kids to come. Write and spell it: _____

    fall = f + **all** (**Fall** rhymes with **ball**.)

    Ooo! Did he **fall?**   Write and spell it: _____

    call = c + **all** (**Call** rhymes with **ball**.)

    I will **call** the dog.   Write and spell it: _____

Read the word list again.

Words for **Zack the Dog** PART 2

• Find the picture that goes with the sentence and draw a line
  to connect them.

Did you **come** to get **some** of the gold?

Jill puts a lock on the **door**.

Bev hits the **ball**. **What** a hit!

Did Cal **fall?** **Call** and ask if he's OK.

All the kids jump in.

Zack the Dog PART 2

Yip! Yip! Yip! Yip!

What is it? Zack sits up.

Zack runs to the back. On the deck sits a pup.

It's his pal, Red! Zack runs to the door.

He wags his tail and jumps up on the door.

Zack just can not be still.

(But you can tell, he's not a bit ill.)

His pal, Red, is back!

He runs and he huffs and he yips.

Up and back, up and back he zips

Till Miss Pim runs in and asks, "What's up?"

As Zack wags his big tail, it hits lots of cups.

O, no! All the cups fall! . . . CRACK!

What a mess! (Can Zack put the cups back?)

Is Zack a mad dog? Is he a bit nuts?

No, Zack is just glad, for he is in luck.

His pal has come back.

(And so at last Zack's *not* a sad sack!)

Did Zack miss his pal? You bet he did.

But Red has come back. She's come back to play.

Zack nods, "Yes, she's come back to stay."

Yes 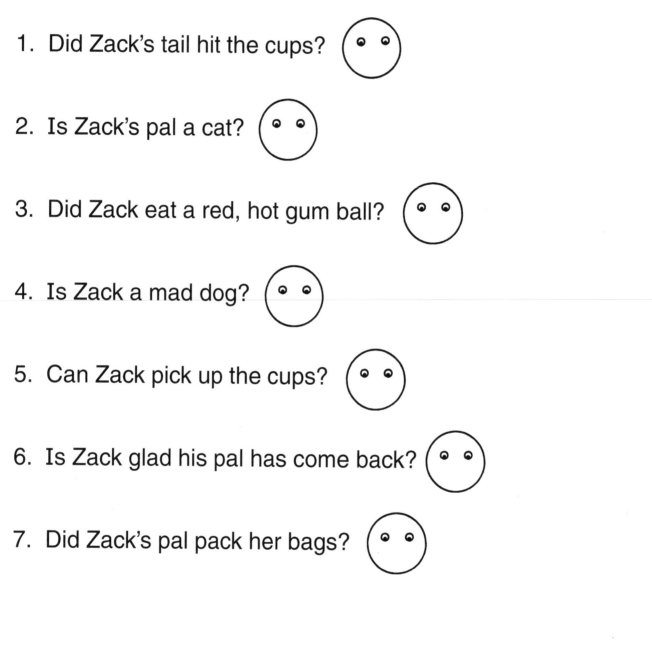 **No** **Can't Tell**

• Draw the face to show the answer.

1. Did Zack's tail hit the cups?

2. Is Zack's pal a cat?

3. Did Zack eat a red, hot gum ball?

4. Is Zack a mad dog?

5. Can Zack pick up the cups?

6. Is Zack glad his pal has come back?

7. Did Zack's pal pack her bags?

What is Zack's pal's name?

_____

- -

_____

18

Put a big tail on Zack, and add 2 or 3 cups to the mess.
Color it.

Think About It!

1. Tell 1 thing that you can miss.

_____

- -

_____

2. Tell 1 thing that can crack but is not an egg.

_____

- -

_____

3. What has a tail but is not a dog?

_____

- -

_____

4. Why did Zack act as if he's a mad dog?

_____

- -

_____

5. What can fall but is not a cup?

_____

- -

_____

6. Tell what to do if a pot of jam falls on the rug.

_____

- -

_____

Can You Figure This Out?

• On each line 4 words go together in some way.
  One word does not fit.
  Circle the word that does not fit.

1.   ball   bat   blocks   doll   (yell)

2.   hand   neck   leg   bag   hip

3.   dog   box   cat   pig   rat

4.   cup   pan   mug   hen   pot

5.   log   kiss   rub   pat   hug

6.   wag   lick   yip   dig   eggs

7.   run   jog   hop   sit   jump

Introduction to **Zack the Dog** PART 3

• Let's read some more contractions.
  Cross out the letters that are left out.

she + i̶s̶ = she's   let + us = let's

I + will = I'll   can + not = can't

I + am = I'm   of the clock = o'clock

• Here are more word families to read.
  Circle the parts that are the same.

rest   ham

best   jam

nest   **s**lam

lock   tell

rock   sell

clock   **s**mell

end

ben**d**

sen**d**

22

Words for **Zack the Dog** PART 3

1. **this** = **This** rhymes with *miss*.

    This man is my dad.   Write and spell it: _____

2. **ear** =

    A dog has 2 **ears.**   Write and spell it: _____

    hear = **Hear** rhymes with **ear.**

    I **hear** the kids yell.   Write and spell it: _____

3. **where** = **Where** rhymes with

    Where is Zack? **Where** did he go?

    Write and spell it: _____

4. **more** = m + or (**More** rhymes with 4.)

    Tad gives Max **more** to eat.

    Write and spell it: _____

5. **with** = wi + the

    Give me a hot dog **with** a bun.

    Write and spell it: _____

6. **from** = f + rum

    Eggs come **from** hens.

    Write and spell it: _____

Read the word list again.

Words for **Zack the Dog** PART 3

• Find the picture that goes with the sentence and draw a line
  to connect them.

Where did **this** big rod come **from**?

My dog has big **ears**.

Liz can not eat a bit **more**.

What do I **hear**?

Fill it **with** gas!

Zack the Dog PART 3

At last Zack's pal has come.

(But we can't tell where from!)

Zack's pal is a mess!

Miss Pim hears the yips and comes on the run.

"Where," she asks Zack, "did this mutt come from?"

"What a mess! It has mud from its top to the tip of its tail.

It's wet, and it smells, and the smell is so bad!

This mutt must go. It must go back.

It's not fit to play with my pup Zack!"

But Miss Pim can not send the dog back.

It has no tag and no I.D.

What can she do?

She's mad as can be!

"No! You can't send Red back!

Red's my pal," yells Zack.

"You must let her stay!" he begs Miss Pim.

"She can eat from my pan, and I'll do what I can.

I'll give her my bed. I'll nap on the cot.

Red's the best pal I've got, and I'd miss her a lot."

Zack begs Miss Pim to let the pup in, but Miss Pim will not!

"No, Zack!" she yells. "It can't come in! It's a mess!

It'll get mud on the rugs, and I'll bet it has bugs!

Be still, Zack! No more!" Miss Pim huffs

As she slams the back door.

Zack can not win. Miss Pim will not let the mutt in.

"Let's go to bed. It's ten o'clock," Miss Pim tells Zack.

"Come, I'll tuck you in."

Zack gets a hug and a kiss as Miss Pim puts him to bed,

But she locks the back door on the sad, wet pup, Red.

At last Miss Pim is off to bed.

Yes 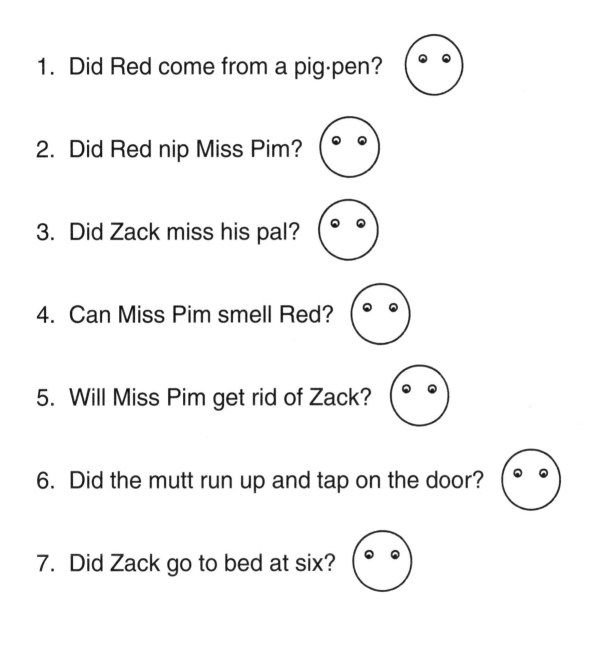 **No** **Can't Tell**

• Draw the face to show the answer.

1. Did Red come from a pig·pen?

2. Did Red nip Miss Pim?

3. Did Zack miss his pal?

4. Can Miss Pim smell Red?

5. Will Miss Pim get rid of Zack?

6. Did the mutt run up and tap on the door?

7. Did Zack go to bed at six?

Tell what you'd be glad to see at your door.

_____

_ _

_____

Put ears on Zack's pal, Red, as she sits on the deck.

Add grass  and flowers. Color it.

Think About It!

1. Name 1 thing that is black.

_____

- -

_____

2. Name 1 thing that can be a mess.

_____

- -

_____

3. What can you hear at the door that is not a dog?

_____

- -

_____

4. "It's not fit to play with my pup" means:

_____

- -

_____

5. Miss Pim did not let Red in. Why?

_____

- -

_____

6. Why can't Miss Pim send Red back?

_____

- -

_____

Can You Figure This Out?

• Write a word that fits the meaning and begins with **B.**

1. A bird   _____blue jay_____

2. A name _____

3. A color _____

4. A vegetable _____

5. A sport _____

6. You can sleep on it. _____

Write one more word that begins with B. _____

32

Means the Opposite

• Read each word in the first list. Find the word in the second list that means the opposite and draw a line to it.

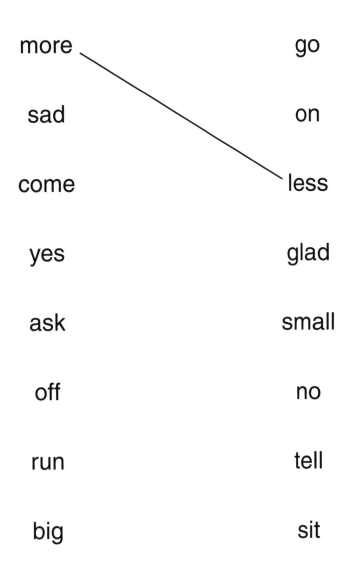

more   go

sad   on

come   less

yes   glad

ask   small

off   no

run   tell

big   sit

Pick a word from the lists and write a sentence.

_____

_ _

_____

Introduction to **Zack the Dog** PART 4

- Let's read some more word families that you will need to know.
  Circle the parts that are the same.

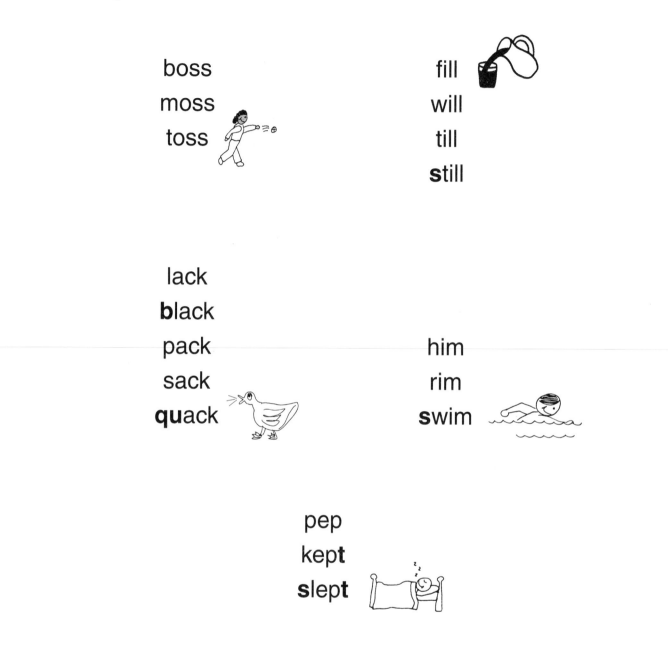

boss
moss
toss

fill
will
till
still

lack
black
pack
sack
quack

him
rim
swim

pep
kept
slept

Words for **Zack the Dog** PART 4

1. **cold** =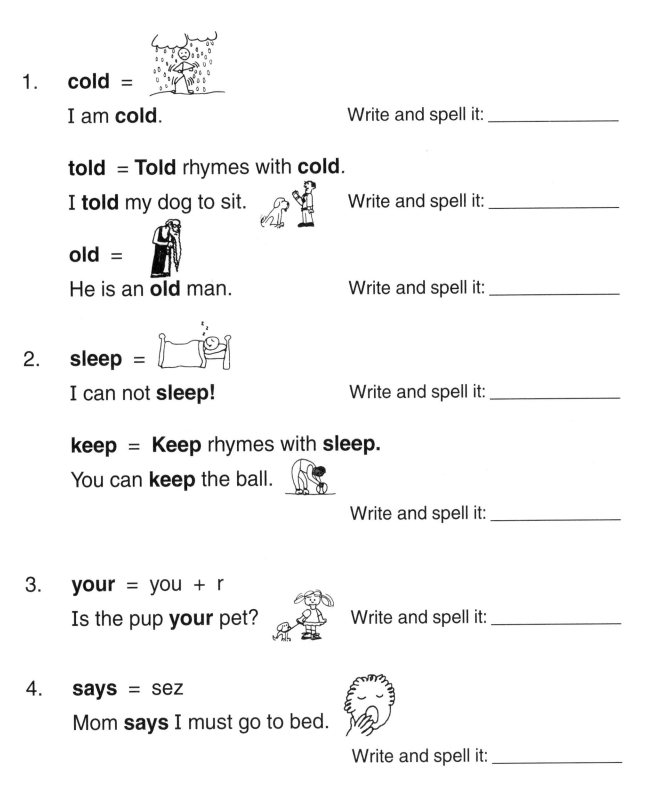

   I am **cold**.   Write and spell it: _____

   told = **Told** rhymes with **cold**.

   I **told** my dog to sit.   Write and spell it: _____

   old =

   He is an **old** man.   Write and spell it: _____

2. **sleep** =

   I can not **sleep**!   Write and spell it: _____

   keep = **Keep** rhymes with **sleep.**

   You can **keep** the ball.

                                       Write and spell it: _____

3. **your** = you + r

   Is the pup **your** pet?   Write and spell it: _____

4. **says** = sez

   Mom **says** I must go to bed.

                                       Write and spell it: _____

Read the word list again.

Words for **Zack the Dog** PART 4

• Find the picture that goes with the sentence and draw a line
  to connect them.

Is this **your** dog?

Nan **told** her pal to call her back.

Val fed the **old** cats.

Dad **says**, "**Keep** still so I can
sleep!"

It's a **cold** day to go for a swim.

Zack the Dog PART 4

Zack is so sad. His pal, Red, is not bad.

But will Red run off, run off and get mad?

Red sits in the cold. What can she do?

She can't run off on her pal, Zack the pup!

So Red stays and yips till the hot sun comes up.

But you can bet Miss Pim is up·set!

"Be still! Stop the fuss!" she calls to Red.

"I'm mad as can be as I toss in my bed.

I can't sleep a bit with your yip, yip, yip!

I'm fed up and mad, so zip up your lip!"

Miss Pim's sick of it, you can tell,

And on top of it all, she has not slept well.

But Miss Pim can not win. Red will not give in.

At last she gets up and un·locks the door.

"Come on in," she says, as she lets the pup in.

"I give up!" Miss Pim tells Red. "OK. You win!

If Zack has a pal, I can tell she's my pal as well."

Yes  **No** **Can't Tell**

• Draw the face to show the answer.

1. Did Miss Pim sleep well?

2. Will Zack miss his pal if she runs off?

3. Did Red yip till Miss Pim got up?

4. Did Miss Pim win a bet with Zack?

5. Will Miss Pim get a pet duck?

6. Is the mutt a black bull·dog?

7. Did Miss Pim let Red come in?

Tell why Red did not run off.

_____

— — — — — — — — — — — — — — — — — — —

_____

Draw more of Miss Pim in her bed.

Add the sun as it comes up.

Think About It!

1. Name 1 thing that is cold.

_____

2. What can keep you from sleep that is not a dog?

_____

3. Where can you sleep that is not a bed?

_____

4. Miss Pim yells, "Zip up your lip!" She means:

_____

5. Why did Miss Pim let Red in at last?

_____

6. Is a dog a good pet? Why?

_____

Can You Figure This Out?

• Add a word to finish the sentence.

1. A dog yips;

   A duck _____quacks_____ .

2. You can fill a sack;

   You can pack a b _____ .

3. A kid will hum;

   A bee will b _____ .

4. A pot has a top;

   A can has a l _____ .

5. Mom gives a kiss;

   A dog gives a l _____ .

6. A sink has suds;

   A can of pop has f_____ .

7. You sit in a chair;

   You sleep in a b _____ .

Introduction to **Zack the Dog** PART 5

• Let's read more contractions. Cross out the letter(s)
  that were left out.

I ãm = I'm   she will = she'll

we are = we're   we will = we'll

I will = I'll   they are = they're

• Read the word families below, and circle the parts that are
  the same.

If you can read **if**, you can read:

tiff   buds

stiff   du**ds**

sniff   su**ds**

cast   rip

fast   **d**rip

last   si**ps**

past   yi**ps**

Words for **Zack the Dog** PART 5

1. **clean** =

   The dog is **clean** at last.   Write and spell it: _____

2. **good** = **Good** means *not bad.*

   This will be **good** to eat.

   Write and spell it: _____

3. **than** = The word *the* + *an*

   He is big·ger **than** you!

   Write and spell it: _____

4. **have** = hav

   I **have** a doll.   Write and spell it: _____

5. **one** = 1

   I have **one** cat.   Write and spell it: _____

6. **two** = 2

   The nest has **two** eggs.

   Write and spell it: _____

Read the word list again.

Words for **Zack the Dog** PART 5

• Find the picture that goes with the sentence and draw a line
  to connect them.

The **two** cats **have** a sip of pop.

Pat gets all **clean** in the suds.

Dad is tall·er **than** I am.

A big hat is **good** in the sun.

Gus has **one** sock to fix.

Zack the Dog PART 5

Miss Pim fills the tub till the tub's full of suds.

Then she picks up the mutt and pops her into the tub.

Miss Pim rubs and rubs so, so fast,

Till Red has no mud, and she's all clean at last.

"Well, well, well! A *red* pup!" Miss Pim yells.

"This dog is *not* black!

At last she is clean, and she smells so good!

What a dog! Red is tip-top!

She stays if I tell her and comes if I call.

Red is not a bad dog at all!"

Miss Pim pats Zack on the back.

"I can't tell a fib! Your pal Red is swell.

She can stay on. She'll be good, I can tell!

And I'll bet," Miss Pim adds, "we'll have lots of fun.

For two pets must be more fun than one!"

So Zack has his pal, and Miss Pim is not mad.

Zack, the dog, is not sad.

Zack, the dog, is not sick.

He gives Miss Pim a big, wet lick!

At last Zack will eat and play and run,

For he has a pal, and it's lots of fun.

Yes  **No** **Can't Tell**

• Draw the face to show the answer.

1. Is Zack a black lab pup?

2. Is Zack still sad?

3. Will Zack get fat?

4. Did Red have fun in the tub?

5. Is Zack's pal, Red, a good dog?

6. Will Miss Pim have 3 pets?

7. Is it fun to have a pal?

What do you and your pal do to have fun?

_____

_ _

_____

Add suds to the tub, and put eyes 👁👁 on Red.
Color it.

Think About It!

1. Name two things you can have fun with.

_____

- -

_____

2. What can get clean in a tub but is not a dog?

_____

- -

_____

3. Name a thing that is red but is not a dog.

_____

- -

_____

4. Tell why Miss Pim lets Red stay.

_____

- -

_____

5. "I can't tell a fib," means:

_____

- -

_____

6. Why can two pets be more fun than one?

_____

- -

_____

Can You Figure This Out?

• The sentences in each group below are in the wrong order.
  Put the sentences in the right order by writing 1, 2, 3 to tell
  which comes first, next, and last.

_____1_____	Pam has a ball to toss.
_____3_____	Pam can't get the ball from the mud.
_____2_____	The ball falls in the mud.
_____	Zack is sad.
_____	His old pal, Red, yips at the door.
_____	Zack runs to the door.
_____	The mutt has mud on him.
_____	The mutt is red at last.
_____	Miss Pim puts the mutt in a tub of suds.
_____	Miss Pim has two dogs.
_____	Miss Pim has no kids.
_____	Miss Pim got no sleep.
_____	Zack's pal comes back.
_____	Zack is sad, for he has no pal.
_____	Zack, Red, and Miss Pim will have fun.
_____	Miss Pim tells Zack that Red has bugs.
_____	Miss Pim puts Red in the tub.
_____	Miss Pim will not let Red in.

Introduction to **Six Kids Jog** PART 1

• Let's read more word families.
  Circle the parts that are the same.

ten   mil**k**
ten**t**   sil**k**
sen**t**

pep   ban**k**   ink
step   yan**k**   win**k**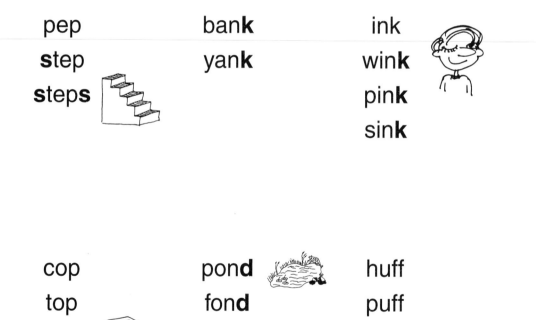
step**s**   pin**k**
                          sin**k**

cop   pon**d**   huff
top   fon**d**   puff
stop   **s**tuff

Words for **Six Kids Jog** PART 1

1. **next** = nex + t

   Ben is **next** to the cat.

   Write and spell it: _____

2. **are** = R

   Are you cold and wet?   Write and spell it: _____

3. **then** = **Then** rhymes with *ten*.

   She packs her bag and **then** locks it.

   Write and spell it: _____

4. **down** = ⇩

   It is not up. It is **down**.   Write and spell it: _____

5. **saw** =

   The **saw** has rust on it.   Write and spell it: _____

6. **they** = **They** rhymes with *play*.

   The kids play. **They** are pals.

   Write and spell it: _____

Read the word list again.

Words for **Six Kids Jog** PART 1

• Find the picture that goes with the sentence and draw a line
 to connect them.

Then they got in·to bed.

We hid in the tent,
but Mom and Dad **saw** us.

Tim sits **next** to his pals, Sal and Bess.

Can you get this one **down** for me?

Are you glad you have a fast van?

Six Kids Jog PART 1

"It's a good day for a jog," says Tess.

"I'll call up my pals and see if they can go for a run."

So Tess calls up her pals, Peg and Bud.

Then she gives Liz a buzz.

Next, she calls Min and Bill to see if they can come.

"What fun!" they all tell Tess. "We're sick of TV!"

So one by one, they come on the run!

The pals get all set to go.

They tuck hats and sun·tan stuff in sacks,

And zip up the six back·packs.

Tess packs ham on buns for all to eat.

Bill lugs a jug of pop with fizz.

He gives the cups to Liz.

It's a hot day to be in the sun,

But the kids can tell it will be fun!

At last the kids pick up the packs.

Peg sets off. The rest are in back.

So Peg is the one to see the cub best!

"Ooo!" She taps her lips and nods to the rest.

Do they see it? They all stop and are still

Till the cub runs off to its den in the rocks.

"What fun! What will it be next?" asks Bill.

Six kids can run and jog in the sun.

Six kids can have a lot of fun.

They eat the ham buns as they run.

They pass a pond, and they're so hot they jump in for a dip!

So hair, feet, legs, socks, all drip, drip, drip . . .

And, you can bet, six back·packs get all wet!

Next, the kids stop for a sip of pop.

Then they pick up and run on and on.

Yes 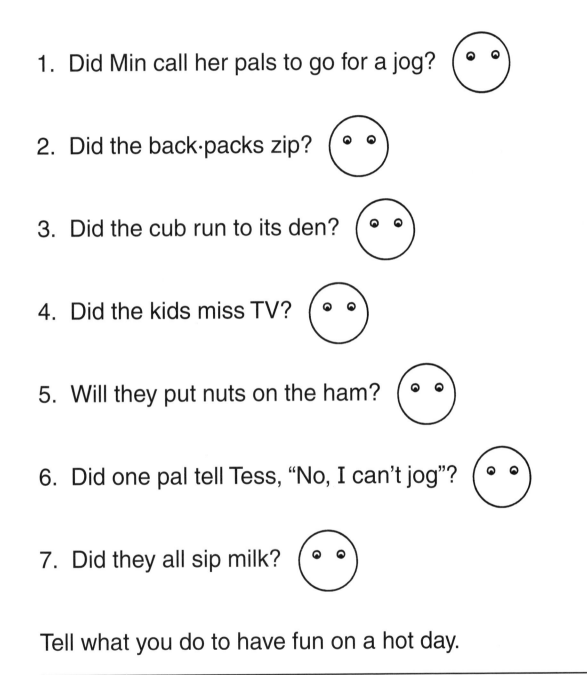 **No** **Can't Tell**

• Draw the face to show the answer.

1. Did Min call her pals to go for a jog?

2. Did the back·packs zip?

3. Did the cub run to its den?

4. Did the kids miss TV?

5. Will they put nuts on the ham?

6. Did one pal tell Tess, "No, I can't jog"?

7. Did they all sip milk?

Tell what you do to have fun on a hot day.

_____

_ _

_____

Draw what the kids had on their backs.

Think About It!

1. Name a thing you can pack that is not a back·pack.

_____

2. Name 2 things that are fun to sip.

_____

3. Name 1 thing that can cut.

_____

4. What gets hot but is not the sun?

_____

5. Why did the kids pack hats and sun·tan stuff?

_____

6. Why did Peg tap her lips af·ter she saw the cub?

_____

Can You Figure This Out?

• On each line 4 words go together in some way.
  One word does not fit.
  Circle the word that does not fit.

1. tea   milk   pop   six   egg·nog

2. fox   tug   pull   yank   drag

3. tell   ask   tin   nag   beg

4. hot   wet   sick   cold   ball

5. ear   leg   hip   bug   lips

6. cat   black   tan   pink   red

7. door   eat   deck   wall   steps

Means the Same

• Here are some more words that mean the same. Draw a line from the word in the first list to the word in the second list that means the same.

sleep	we
says	clean
smell	fill
us	cup
mop	tells
pack	nap
jump	sniff
mug	hop

Pick a word from the lists and write a sentence.

_____

— —

_____

Introduction to **Six Kids Jog** PART 2

• Read the contractions below.
  Cross out the letters that are left out.

you + will = you'll   let + us = let's

they + will = they'll   I + am = I'm

• Read the word families you will meet next.

bell   tin

belt   grin

felt   win

melt   wind

jock   pass

locks   past

rocks   gas

socks   grass

Words for **Six Kids Jog** PART 2

1. **feet** =

    My **feet** are big.   Write and spell it: _____

2. **was** = wuz

    The pot **was** so hot!   Write and spell it: _____

3. **hair** =

    Pat has red **hair**.   Write and spell it: _____

4. **tree** =

    The cat is up in the **tree**.   Write and spell it: _____

    see = **See** rhymes with **tree**.

    I can **see** you.   Write and spell it: _____

    free = **Free** rhymes with **tree**.

    The dog is not **free** to run.

    Write and spell it: _____

Read the word list again.

Words to Help You Read **Six Kids Jog** PART 2

• Find the picture that goes with the sentence, and draw a line
  to connect them.

He has no **hair**.

Val **was** mad she did not win.

The bug has six **feet**.

We got in **free** and had lots of fun.

He can **see** rocks and **trees**
and a lot more.

Six Kids Jog PART 2

So on and on the kids ran.

Peg still led the pack, and Bill was in back.

Then Liz ran by Peg, and so did Bud.

But as Bud ran past Peg, he fell and hit a rock,

Got a cut on his leg, and mud on his sock.

What bad luck Bud had! All the kids felt so bad.

Bud sat down to rest by a tree.

Was he OK? The kids ran up to see.

Did Bud fuss or sob? No! No! No!

Bud got up fast. "I'm not a jock, as you can see!

But I'm OK. So let's go!" he told the kids.

"Come jog with me."

"Let's see if one of us can win!" Tess told the kids.

Tess ran and ran till she ran past Min.

But Min had no pep, and she had no wind.

(Tess will be the one to win!)

Min's feet felt so bad, but she did not give up.

Huff! Puff! She was so hot, but she did not stop!

Was Min the last to get up to the top?

By two o'clock the kids had all come back.

They sat down on the grass to pull off the packs.

They felt so hot and they had to rest.

But they'll tell you, if you ask, "A jog with pals is the best!"

So pick a good day and call up your pals.

Then fill up your packs and set off for a run.

I bet you'll have lots of fun as you jog in the sun.

Yes  **No** **Can't Tell**

• Draw the face to show the answer.

1. Is Bud a jock?

2. Did the kids run past a pond?

3. Did ten kids jump in for a dip?

4. Are the back·packs a wet mess?

5. Did the ham buns get wet?

6. Did Tess get up the hill?

7. Did Min give up?

Write the name of the kid that had bad luck.

_____

_ _

_____

Draw more of Min as she gets to the top of the hill.
Give her a grin and a big sun hat.

Think About It!

1. Name one thing that can drip.

_____

- -

_____

2. What is wet but is not a pond?

_____

- -

_____

3. What can you go down that is not a hill?

_____

- -

_____

4. Tell what you can see as you jog that is not a cub.

_____

- -

_____

5. If a bun gets wet, it will be:

_____

- -

_____

6. What will you do if you cut your leg on a rock?

_____

- -

_____

Can You Figure This Out?

• Finish the sentences below with words
that rhyme with the boldface words.

1. Six kids can have **fun**.
   Six kids can jog in the ___sun___.

2. The kids will put stuff in **sacks**
   and zip up the back _____.

3. Peg led the **pack.**
   The rest ran in _____.

4. Bud sat down by a **tree.**
   The kids all ran up to _____.

5. Did Bud yell, "**No**"?
   He said, "Let's _____!"

6. Tess ran past **Min**.
   Tess will be the one to _____.

7. Can Min get up the **hill**?
   You can bet that she _____.

Means the Opposite

• Read each word in the first list. Find the word in the second row
  that means the opposite and draw a line to it.

stop	down
sick	out
cold	go
up	keep
in	feet
give	well
back	hot
hands	front

Pick a word from the lists and write a sentence.

_____

_ _

_____

Introduction to **Help! 911** PART 1

• Here are more word families to help you read **Help! 911**.
Read them aloud and circle the parts that are the same.

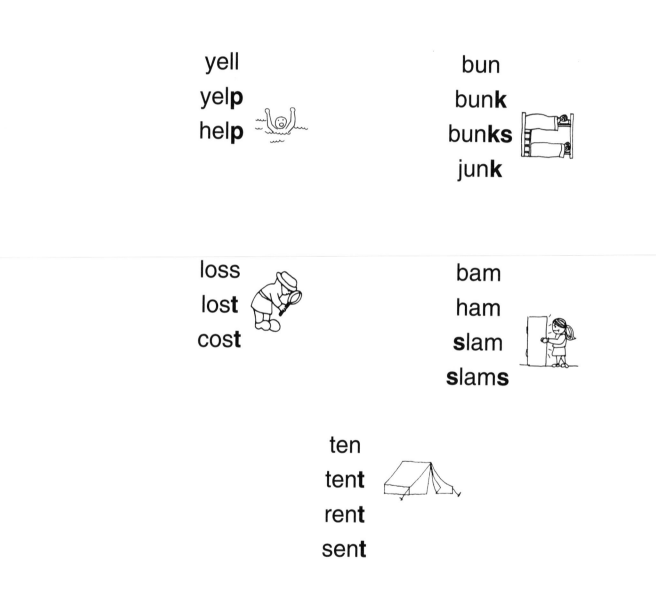

yell
yel**p**
hel**p**

bun
bunk
bunks
ju**n**k

loss
los**t**
cos**t**

bam
ham
slam
slam**s**

ten
tent
rent
sent

Words for **Help! 911** PART 1

1. **book** =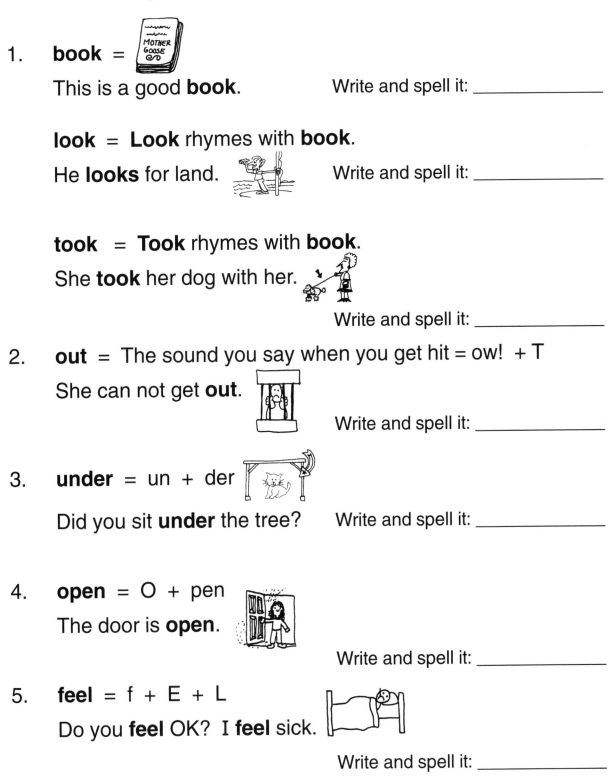

   This is a good **book**.   Write and spell it: _____

   look = **Look** rhymes with **book**.

   He **looks** for land.   Write and spell it: _____

   took = **Took** rhymes with **book**.

   She **took** her dog with her.

   Write and spell it: _____

2. **out** = The sound you say when you get hit = ow! + T

   She can not get **out**.

   Write and spell it: _____

3. **under** = un + der

   Did you sit **under** the tree?   Write and spell it: _____

4. **open** = O + pen

   The door is **open**.

   Write and spell it: _____

5. **feel** = f + E + L

   Do you **feel** OK? I **feel** sick.

   Write and spell it: _____

Read the word list again.

Words for **Help! 911** PART 1

• Find the picture that goes with the sentence, and draw a line
  to connect them.

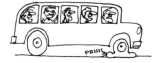

Look! A bug hid **under** the tent.

Ted is mad that he **took** the bus.

Oooo! No! He's **out**! They win!

Meg will **open** the box from Pat.
Is it a **book**?

Rex **feels** hot.

Help! 911 PART 1

The sun is up, but Todd and Em do not get up.

They just got bunk beds, and it's lots of fun to be in bunks!

Em's bed is on top, for she is six. (Todd is just 3!)

Em and Todd stay in bed and look at books.

It's fun to be in bed with a book!

But Em has lost her best one.

Where can it be? She runs off to see.

Todd gets up to help Em look.

Let me see! Where can the book be? Then he sees it!

"Come and look, Em! I have it!" Todd calls.

"It's under the bed!"

"You're a big help," Em tells him as she comes back.

But just then the door slams. BAM!

Todd tugs on it, but as he tugs, it locks!

So Todd is *in*, and Em is *out*.

O! NO! Todd can't get the door open.

O! NO! Em can't get the door open.

Todd gets mad and kicks the door.

"Let me out!" he yells. BAM! BAM! BAM!

Em feels so bad. What can she do?

What if Todd can't get out? What will he do?

Yes 🙂 **No** ☹ **Can't Tell** 😐

• Draw a face to show the answer.

1. Did the kids get up with the sun? ◯

2. Did the kids see TV in bed? ◯

3. Did Todd help Em? ◯

4. Was the lost book under the bed? ◯

5. Did Todd tug on his bunk bed? ◯

6. Did the wind slam the door? ◯

7. Did Todd kick a ball? ◯

Write the name of the book you like best.

_____

_ _

_____

Draw more of the kids in the bunk beds
and add lots of books.

Think About It!

1. Name two things that can lock.

   _____

   -

   _____

2. What can be lost that is not a book?

   _____

   -

   _____

3. What can you look under that is not a bed?

   _____

   -

   _____

4. Why did Todd help Em?

   _____

   -

   _____

5. Tell where you can go to look for a lost book.

   _____

   -

   _____

6. What can you do to help a pal?

   _____

   -

   _____

Can You Figure This Out?

• The words on each line rhyme.
  Think of one more word that rhymes
  and write it on the line.

1.   she   we   bee   _____

2.   rock   dock   jock   _____

3.   pops   mops   tops   _____

4.   all   fall   hall   _____

5.   lick   nick   tick   _____

6.   fog   bog   log   _____

7.   took   hook   cook   _____

Introduction to **Help! 911** PART 2

• Read the following word families from **Help! 911**.
  Circle the parts that are the same.

If you can read **miss**, you can read:

mist
list
fist

in**k**
rin**k**
drink

an**d**
lan**d**
han**d**
han**ds**

cap
map
tap
lap
clap

lick
pick
sick
quick
trick

Words for **Help! 911** PART 2

1. **cry** =

    He did not **cry** a lot.

    Write and spell it: _____

    my = **My** rhymes with **cry**.

    My pet can not get out.

    Write and spell it: _____

    try = **Try** rhymes with **cry**.

    I will **try** to win.

    Write and spell it: _____

2. **brave** = **Brave** rhymes with .

    He is **brave**.

    Write and spell it: _____

3. **begin** = be + gin

    He **begins** his run.

    Write and spell it: _____

4. **room** = **Room** rhymes with .

    My **room** is a mess.

    Write and spell it: _____

Read the word list again.

Words for **Help! 911** PART 2

• Find the picture that goes with the sentence, and draw a line
  to connect them.

"Go to your **room!**" Mom tells Jack.

Jill is **brave** to be in the tree.

I hug **my** doll.

If you **begin** to **cry**, so will I.

Dev will **try** to eat the big hot dog.

Help! 911 PART 2

As Todd begins to cry, Em runs to get Mom.

"Help! Mom! Come quick!" Em yells.

"Todd's in the bed·room and can't get out!"

Mom comes on the run.

She tugs on the door. She asks Todd if he's OK.

"NO!" Todd yells. "I'm not OK! I can't get out!"

Mom tugs and tugs, but she can't get the door open.

Dad comes and tells Todd to pull the lock up.

Todd pulls, but he can not get the lock free.

(He's just 3, you see!)

Then Em begins to cry.

Todd begins to hit the door with his fist,

And then to cry and cry!

They all feel so bad. What can they do?

Todd sobs, and then Em sobs.

What can they do?

Mom tells Dad to call 911 so help will come.

She tells Todd he's OK. Dad tells Todd to be brave.

Em tells him to look at a book for a bit.

But Todd just sobs and has a fit!

At last the cops come and pick the lock.

They get the door open and Todd runs out.

Mom, Dad, and Em all hug Todd and tell him he's brave.

Todd hops up and down and claps his hands.

He is so glad to see the cops.

From then on, cops are tops!

And Todd tells all he can see,

"I'll be a cop one day and set kids free!"

Yes 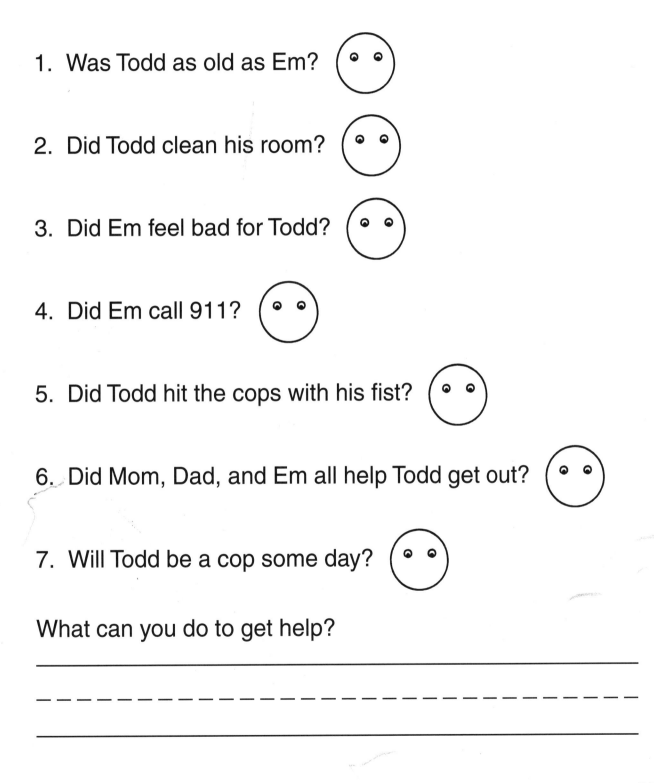 **No** **Can't Tell**

• Draw the face to show the answer.

1. Was Todd as old as Em?

2. Did Todd clean his room?

3. Did Em feel bad for Todd?

4. Did Em call 911?

5. Did Todd hit the cops with his fist?

6. Did Mom, Dad, and Em all help Todd get out?

7. Will Todd be a cop some day?

What can you do to get help?

_____

_ _

_____

Draw more of Todd after the door is open.

Think About It!

1. Name two things you can tug on.

_____

\- \-

_____

2. What is OK to hit with your fist?

_____

\- \-

_____

3. What can you open that is not a door?

_____

\- \-

_____

4. Tell why Em begins to cry.

_____

\- \-

_____

5. What can you do if you're in a room and can't get out?

_____

\- \-

_____

6. Todd will be a cop some day. What will you be?

_____

\- \-

_____

Can You Figure This Out?

• Write a word that fits and begins with M.

1. an animal _____monkey_____

2. what you can put milk in _____

3. a thing in the sky _____

4. a drink _____

5. a word that means angry _____

6. what you can put on your hand _____

Write one more word that begins with M. _____

Words Introduced in Beyond The Code 1

all	eat	next	then
are	fall	old	they
ball	feel	one	this
begin	feet	open	told
book	free	out	took
brave	from	play	tree
call	give	room	try
clean	good	saw	two
cold	hair	says	under
come	have	see	was
cry	hear	sleep	what
day	keep	some	where
door	look	stay	why
down	more	tail	with
ear	my	than	your